Pirate School

Written by Lisa Thompson
Pictures by Craig Smith and Lew Keilar

A pirate's life is full of surprises. When Barnacle Bill came aboard, the crew of The Black Beast got a huge surprise. Barnacle Bill was the head of the Pirate School ship and he wasn't happy.

3

"Whirling whales!" said Barnacle Bill. "What kind of pirates are you? You have forgotten how to be bold, fierce, and nasty pirates. It's back to school for the lot of you."

"Pirate School?" said Red Beard and his crew.

"Yes. Now get to your lessons," yelled Barnacle Bill.

There were lots of classes at Pirate School. First, was sword-fighting class.

Captain Red Beard cut his finger. He did not like the sight of blood. His legs went wobbly. His crew got wobbly legs, too.

"I think I need to go to sick bay," Captain Red Beard said.

Barnacle Bill shook his head and raised his sword.

"What kind of pirates are you?" he cried.

Then, there was cannon-firing class.

The Captain's red beard got burned when the cannon fired. Black soot covered the crew.

"Now you're looking like a crew of fierce pirates!" said Colin, the cannon master.

Barnacle Bill just shook his head.

"What kind of pirates are you?" he cried.

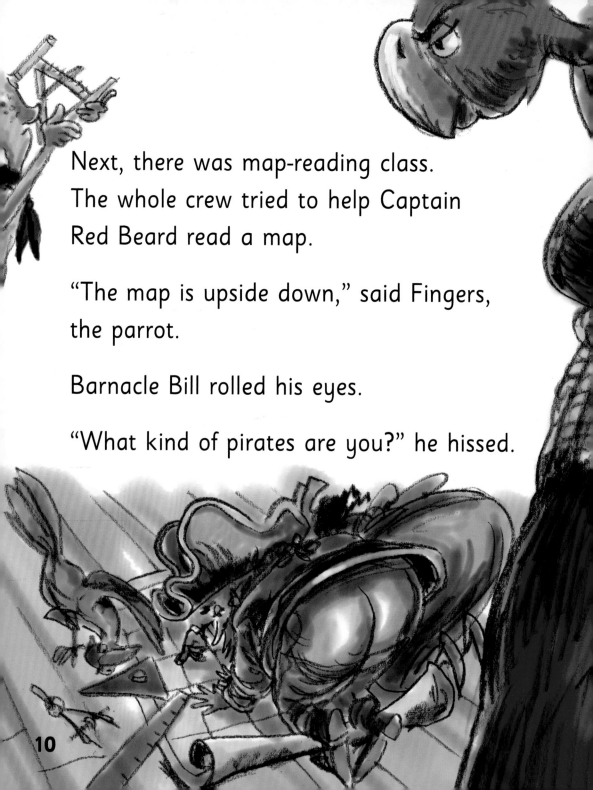

Next, there was map-reading class.
The whole crew tried to help Captain
Red Beard read a map.

"The map is upside down," said Fingers,
the parrot.

Barnacle Bill rolled his eyes.

"What kind of pirates are you?" he hissed.

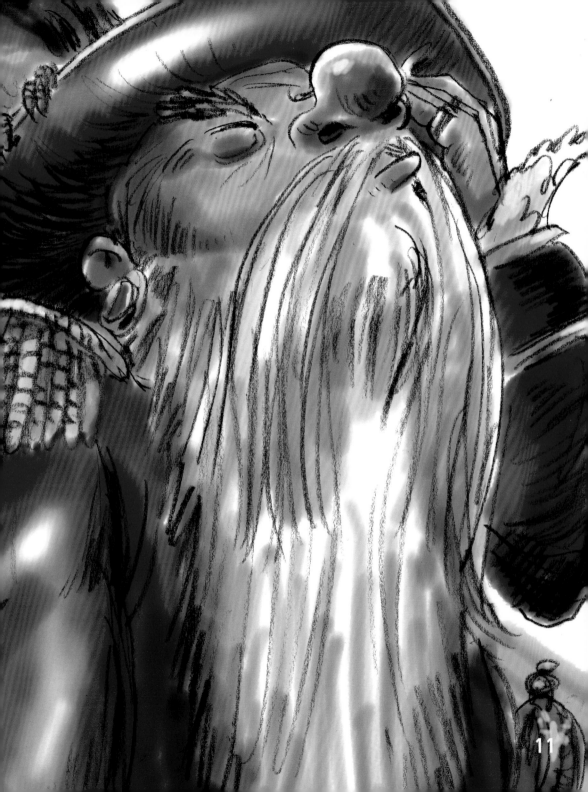

"Try using the compass," said Bones, the dog.

Lizzie pointed at the windvane. She told the Captain how it worked.

"How interesting," said Captain Red Beard.

Barnacle Bill gritted his teeth.

"What kind of pirates are you?" he snarled.

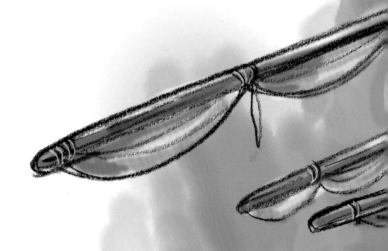

On Thursday, they had pirate band practice.
The Captain and the crew were very bad.

The teachers hid in the sails and barrels to
get away from the noise.

Captain Red Beard ordered his crew to play
even louder. "Now this is music!" he said.

Barnacle Bill did not think so. He was
having an afternoon nap. He stormed out
onto the deck. He was about to explode.

"What kind of pirates are you?"
he screamed.

Treasure-sharing class was on Friday.
The crew were all happy to go to this class.

Captain Red Beard was not very good at
adding or subtracting. His sharing skills
were also very bad. His teacher almost
walked the plank!

That night, Captain Red Beard and his crew remembered how to be pirates. They showed Barnacle Bill exactly what kind of pirates they were. Quickly and quietly, they set to work.

"Thanks for the treasure!" shouted Captain Red Beard.

"And the treasure map," cried Lizzie, the first mate.

"You see, we are bold, fierce, and clever pirates," shouted Captain Red Beard. The crew all cheered as they sailed away.

"I think it's better to be a clever pirate than a nasty one," smiled Captain Red Beard. He jumped into his hammock and went to sleep.